WEAPONS OF
MASS DESTRUCTION

WEAPONS OF MASS DESTRUCTION

A simple guide to Spiritual Warfare

CHERYL BACON

Copyright © 2020 by Cheryl Bacon.

Library of Congress Control Number:		2020919445
ISBN:	Hardcover	978-1-6641-3516-1
	Softcover	978-1-6641-3515-4
	eBook	978-1-6641-3514-7

All rights reserved. No part of this book may be reproduced or transmitted in any form or by any means, electronic or mechanical, including photocopying, recording, or by any information storage and retrieval system, without permission in writing from the copyright owner.

The views expressed in this work are solely those of the author and do not necessarily reflect the views of the publisher, and the publisher hereby disclaims any responsibility for them.

Scripture quotations marked KJV are from the Holy Bible, King James Version (Authorized Version). First published in 1611. Quoted from the KJV Classic Reference Bible, Copyright © 1983 by The Zondervan Corporation.

The Holy Bible, Berean Study Bible, BSB
Copyright ©2016, 2018 by Bible Hub
Used by Permission. All Rights Reserved Worldwide.

Any people depicted in stock imagery provided by Getty Images are models, and such images are being used for illustrative purposes only. Certain stock imagery © Getty Images.

Print information available on the last page.

Rev. date: 10/08/2020

To order additional copies of this book, contact:
Xlibris
844-714-8691
www.Xlibris.com
Orders@Xlibris.com
818648

Contents

Acknowledgment vii
Foreword xi
Introduction to Spiritual Warfare xix

Chapter 1 Basic Training 1
Chapter 2 The Dressing Room 11
Chapter 3 Zeroing Your Weapon 21
Chapter 4 Armed and Dangerous 29
Chapter 5 Demonaic Rank and Orders 35
Chapter 6 Shut Your Trap and Open Your Mouth ... 45
Chapter 7 Don't Just Stand There. Pray Something. ... 51

References 59

Acknowledgment

To my son Corrie and my daughter Cierra,

Thank you for allowing me to spend countless hours developing my prayer life. You have walked through the valley of the shadow of death with me and held my hand every step of the way. Even when you did not know what to say, "You were present!" I will never forget you getting mad because I would burst in your room praying all times of night. My response will always be, "Don't bite the hand that feeds you, don't burn the bridge that brought you over, and don't kick the knees that prayed you through!" I love you both from the bottom of my heart to the balcony of my soul! As I always tell you, "We don't get to pick what family we are in! May God continue to keep you, and may you never forget *the power of a praying mother*!"

To my six spiritual brothers Byron, Taylor, Terry, Rommel, Jeffrey, and Wesley,

I am so grateful for your kindness as you allowed me fifteen wonderful years of intercession with your mother, Apostle Ethel Mitchell.

To my sister Wanda,

You have been my sounding board and voice of reason. Thank you for always taking the time to listen to the messages, prayers, and encouraging words. Even though you are the eldest, you still remain open for Godly advice! I love you, sis!

What can I say to you and about you, Mary Anita (Sissy) Reid?

My love for you is like the love Jonathan had for David. You have been my spiritual anchor, prayer partner, teacher, and best friend for over twenty-three years. As God told us in prayer, we are spiritual twin towers and heavy hitters. Like, I told you, we will always remain friends because you know too much about me! May God continue to use you for his glory and may the anointing on your life continue to impact nations!

To the late Apostle Ethel Mitchel,

Words cannot express how grateful I am for your spiritual footing that was steeped in prayer. You have developed me into the prayer warrior and intercessory that I am today. I recall the shut-ins, prayer vigils, fasting, and casting out demons as we walked the streets of Lithonia, Decatur, Atlanta, and Florida and witnessed to countless lost souls until our feet hurt. Your hunger for the presence of God has been and will continue to be my motivational drive. Thank you for being the example of true righteousness and holiness. You did not have a prayer life but a life of prayer! I miss and love you very much!

To first spiritual father, mentor, and leader Bishop Keith Young,

After over eighteen years of walking side by side with you as one of the house prophetess, elder and leader, I have learned that hearing the voice of God requires that I stay close. Thank you for pushing me out my comfort zone and stretching me beyond my limits. You saw things in me that only God could have shown you. Thank you for trusting the God in me! I love you with the love of the Lord!

My leaders Apostle Travis Jennings and Pastor Stephanie Jennings,

Never in my life did I think of writing a book of this caliber. Your strategic and cutting-edge leadership and ministry has caused me to go where I could only dream of. Thank you for that extra push, encouraging words of prophesy that allowed me to launch out into the deep! Thank you for the impartation and apostolic investment into the kingdom of God! May the Lord continue to use you for the upbuilding of his kingdom and glory! I am excited to see what God has to say next! I love you both!

Foreword

I want to personally recommend and endorse *Weapons of Mass Destruction* by Cheryl Bacon. This new book on prayer and spiritual warfare will give you insight and revelation that will shift your life. Cheryl has authentically pressed into this realm for many years. Her prayer life, biblical studies and obedience to God has truly given her supernatural insight. Her knowledge on the subject has come from personal experience and seeing others set free.

In this book, you will be challenged, stretched and strengthened. I want you to know that you have put your hands on an amazing manuscript. As I began to read the pages of this book, I saw a warrior that has been on the frontline naturally and spiritually. This book is birth out of years of experience in dealing with and breaking through difficult problems and strongholds. This book is sure to reveal new heights and deeper depths in the spirit realm. I want to challenge those reading this book to draw from the wisdom given by our Heavenly Father through Cheryl Bacon. Cherish this book as it will be a treasure in your spiritual library.

I believe that many believers will be able to take the practical steps in this book and apply it to their prayer lives. Prayer is essential in God's kingdom and spiritual warfare is real. Knowing how to effectively move in the spiritual realm is very important for the believer's success. You need to understand how to guard yourself and know how to use your weapons. Just like in a natural army, you must know your assignment and your rank. Believers, there is an order to God's kingdom! We must learn how to unify and call for back-up. You must know what you are dealing with and deal with it according.

Cheryl has served faithfully at the Harvest Tabernacle Church for several years. I am amazed at the wisdom she has and her desire to share with others. I know Cheryl's life and her commitment to the Word of God; her foundation in the Lord is strong. Believe me when I tell you, she is equipped to educate.

Daughter, I want to congratulate you for fulfilling the assignment God has given you in the Kingdom and sharing your anointing and dedication with the world. May God continue to bless you as you rise to a new horizon and do greater exploits in the name of Jesus Christ.

My prayer to every reader is that as you read this book, God will give you understanding in all things. Do not be afraid to launch out into the deep. I believe that many breakthroughs will happen in your life as you gain an understanding. Get ready to increase in wisdom and execution of Holy Spirit as you read *Weapons of Mass Destruction*.

Apostle Travis Jennings
Senior Leader, The Harvest Tabernacle Church
Lithonia, GA

What a pleasure it is to write the foreword for this book. After reading *Weapons of Mass Destruction*, I believe the substance within its pages will help you better comprehend the subject of spiritual warfare; in relation to the spiritual battles we face in our personal lives, in our world, and how to *'war a good warfare'* (1 Timothy 1:18).

In *Weapons of Mass Destruction*, Cheryl A. Bacon, has drawn from her military experience to give insight to the spiritual battles we encounter and how to prepare for them. Over the years, I have witnessed both the grace and intensity Cheryl has conducted her life and call as a minister, in the roles of an Intercessor and Prophet.

Weapons of Mass Destruction should be read by serious-minded people. If you are serious about learning how to prepare for your battles, put on the proper armor, learn your assignments, your enemy's tactics, proper use of your weapons, and how to go on the offensive—then you are reading the right book!

As an Apostolic leader, it is my intention to continue to read it regularly for greater insight and I encourage you to do the same!

Apostle Sebastian Weaver Sr.
Faith1ˢᵗ Ministries, Inc.
Douglasville, Georgia

I have known Minister Cheryl Bacon for more than 25 years. Her understanding of the scripture and the Body of Christ has always amazed me. I recommend that you consider purchasing her book, <u>Weapons of Mass Destruction.</u> We are living in a time where so many have questions. Why am I going through this? How am I to get through this? How do I fight my way out of this? At last, Cheryl provides answers to each question, equipping the reader with a full understanding of the weapons that God has given to them as kingdom minded believers, and will qualify them for any warfare that they will be confronted with in their spiritual walk with the Lord. Whether the warfare be in your family, work, or financial, <u>Weapons of Mass Destruction</u> provides you with the kingdom artillery needed to fight any situation. Cheryl has always been a diehard student of the Bible, and therefore I highly recommend that you add this book to your library.

Bishop Keith Young Sr.,
Founder of Vision For Souls Family Worship Center Cathedral
Austell, GA

Twenty-one and fancy free, at least that is what I thought it would be when I finally turned the big twenty-one years of age. After living under strict rules and regulations set forth by my parent, I was ready to live my life the way I wanted to. That exciting time came when I went away to college. I was that college student who understood she needed to get good grades to be successful but still there was a lot of partying to be done.... You know how college students are. Well, I had my fun and along the course of my junior year I became pregnant with my first child. My parents were disappointed as would be expected but I, on the other had the attitude that "I can handle this, it's only a baby".

8 months later this optimistic mother to be, ended up having to be induced due to Pre-eclampsia, which is a pregnancy complication characterized by high blood pressure. Fear started to grip my soul because at this time my baby inside of me did not weight enough to come into this world without needing assistance to survive. Fast forward, I gave birth to a beautiful baby girl who was born fighting for her life. She started to have seizures at 3 months old and other disabilities accompanied this diagnosis of Epilepsy that she was given. She had complications with feeding, being on multiple medications that had to be administered at home via an IV port in heart. And had to have multiple brain surgeries. Can I tell you, this once confident woman who stated at the announcement of my pregnancy "I can handle this" was now feeling like she was in all-out war, fighting for

the life of her child and any chance of possible normalcy our family would have. Little did I know at the time I was in a battle that I was unprepared to fight in the natural as well as in the spirit.

I believe the good Lord heard my heart of pain because at that time I was not a person that prayed much, I barely went to church and really only knew of God from what others mentioned or what I saw them demonstrate. One evening I was encouraged to attend a church service which I brought my daughter along because I was really at a place of desperation. My daughter was having 30-40 seizure per day. We were not sleeping; she had a personal room at the hospital that they kept ready for her arrival at least that is what it seemed like to me. I needed help. During this particular church service my daughter started to go into a seizure and we just so happen to be sitting next to this woman who at that time did not know me nor my child but I quickly realized she was heaven sent to change the very trajectory of our lives. This woman was Cheryl Bacon, the author of this life changing manual you are about to engage in. As my daughter started to go into a seizure this woman Cheryl reached her gentle hand out to touch my daughter and begin to pray. Immediately the seizure stopped, and my daughter's body begin to relax. It was at that moment I realized that there was some untapped power that I was lacking, and I wanted it.

I started to spend more and more time with Cheryl, she started to spend more and more time with my daughter, and eventually becoming my daughters God mother. I learned about her military background and how she was trained to a fight and be ready to defend this country in the time of war. What was so fascinating about Cheryl that I learned during our times together was that she was not only trained in natural war tactics but also trained in a level of spiritual warfare that at the time was beyond my understand. She took me under her wing and taught me that we are in a real war spiritually and naturally. She always insisted that I had to be prepared and always ready to engage because we are fighting against real enemies in the natural as well as in the spirit. Ultimately the enemies marching orders are to steal, kill, and destroy us. Wow…is what you might be saying right now and rightfully so. When we come to understand this realization, it can be a bit intimidating but it brings to our attention that there is an urgency for us to prepared to fight the battles that we will encounter in this life. What Cheryl did from me during my battle of fighting for my daughter's life and our normalcy, she will do for you as you begin to navigate the pages of this book. Because of the training and mentorship, I experienced from Cheryl, I now know how to dress for spiritual battle. My stance is always a position of being ready, watchful, and prayerful. I know who I am, and I know how powerful I am when I follow my commander in chief (Our Heavenly Father) tactical commands and orders. Because of her keen understand of the enemies plans and her sharp understanding of biblical and kingdom principles, she was able to launch me into the place I now stand 25 years later. I am now trained, equipped and ready to engage in battles that I know I will win because I possess the kingdom's weapons of mass destructions.

-Michelle A. Johnson, Founder of
My Moment Outreach Ministries Inc.

WHEN GOD WANTS TO DRILL A MAN!

Rev. Henry Francis Lite (1793-1847)
When God wants to drill a man
And thrill a man, and skill a man;
When God wants to mold a man
To play the noblest part;
When he yearns with all his heart
To create so great and bold a man
That all the world shall be amazed—
Watch his methods, watch his ways
How he ruthlessly perfects
Who he royally elects!
How he hammers him and humbles him
And with mighty blows converts him
Into trials shapes of clay which
Only God understands,
While his tortured heart
Is crying and he lifts beseeching
Hands! How he bends but never
Breaks when his good he undertakes:
How he uses whom he chooses and
With every purpose fuse him,
By every act induces him to try
His splendor out God knows what
He is all about!

THE BLOODY TRUTH

After over twenty-nine years of experiencing and teaching spiritual warfare, I have realized how the military has played a significant role in helping me understand Satan's army. While writing this book, I went through some of the greatest warfare of my life. The attacks came from every side (loss of loved ones, sickness, financial struggle, and nearly losing my children, just to name a few). Trust me, this has been a life lesson and not a story I have read. My prayer is that it will help others learn spiritual warfare by applying the principles and strategy to walk in victory. Then suddenly, in the heat of the battle, God spoke. *"Have not I commanded thee? Be strong of a good courage, be not afraid, neither be thou dismayed; for the Lord thy God is with thee whithersoever thou goest! (Joshua 1:9, King James Version of the Bible) Then the Lord put forth his hand and touched my mouth.* And the Lord said unto me, "Behold, I have put my words in thy mouth, *Now write the book!"*

Introduction to Spiritual Warfare

Even though the United States has embarked upon a war, we as saints are already at war. No bombs fall, no guns are fired, and there are no physical causalities, yet there is great violence. *Until the days of John, the Baptist, until now the Kingdom of Heaven suffereth violence, and the violence take it by force (Matthew 11:12, KJV).* Like it or not, there is a war going on in the heavenlies, but we can actually do something to change the eternal outcome of our battle.

Although we walk in the flesh, we do not war in the flesh, for the weapons of our warfare are not carnal, but they are mighty through God to the pulling down of strongholds. Therefore, we cast down every imagination and every high thing that exalted itself against the knowledge of God and bringing into captivity every thought to the obedience of Christ (2 Corinthians 10:3-5, KJV).

Or what king, going to make war against another king, sitteth not down first, and consulteth whether he be able with ten thousand to meet him that cometh against him with twenty thousand? (Luke 14:31, KJV). Yes, living for Christ is costly, but he already paid the price, and the war has already been won, but we still must fight. Being a soldier is not an option. It is our only choice. When we are born again, we were born into battle and spiritual adversity. We must understand that the battles never stop. We must stand in the righteousness of Jesus Christ and declare that the battle is not ours, but the battle belongs to the Lord.

Nothing from God comes without a fight. Do you think that a person would just let you walk into his house and take their stuff without a fight? We all know that the devil comes to steal, kill, and destroy, but it is our job to get violent in the spirit and fight the devil with our mighty weapons. The spiritual artillery that we possess can unleash more power than any weapon ever designed by man. A weapon without ammunition is useless. Why even join the army of the Lord if you're not going to prepare for battle? Many times, as saints, we make it easy for the enemy because we come to battle unprepared to fight (not prayed-up, not fasting, and unlearned in the word of God), causing us to lie down and die to our situation and circumstances. We often declare that "I am too tired and too old to fight" when you have no choice but to fight. Don't be a poodle saint, barking a couple of times and running for cover! We must be a pit bull in the spirit! Bite down and don't let go until your prey is dead! Well, if you do not get spiritually fit, you will not be able to withstand the spiritual fight. Even though God had equipped us with great resources for battle, we must remember that we will not be successful if we are a divided army. For a house divided against itself shall not stand. We must unify our resistance in order to win the battle. So why not join forces and whip the devil's butt. *For one can chase a thousand and two can chase ten thousand (Deuteronomy 32:30, KJV). Now let's get fit for battle!*

LAWS OF WARFARE

When thou goest out to battle against thine enemies, and seest horses, and chariots, and a people more than thou, be not afraid of them; for the Lord thy God is with thee, which brought thee up out of the land Egypt. And it shall be, when ye are come nigh unto the battle, that the priest shall approach and speak unto the people, And shall say unto them, Hear, O Israel, ye approach this day unto battle against your enemies; let not yours hearts faint, fear not, and do not tremble, neither be terrified because of them. For the Lord your God is he that goeth with you, to fight for you against your enemies, to save you.

—Deuteronomy 20:1-4, KJV)

Plainly stated,

1. Don't be afraid of the enemy.
2. Don't be afraid to fight. Don't punk out or back down!
3. God's got your back, but you still got to fight!
4. Now let's go to war!

CHAPTER ONE

Basic Training

For bodily exercise profiteth little, but godliness is profitable unto all thing having promise of the life that now is, and of that which is to come.

—1 Timothy 4:8, KJV

At the young age of nineteen, I joined the US Army, not for reasons most people do! My motive for leaving my hometown was to avoid marrying my high school sweetheart. We both were young and I wanted to experience life without being tied down. I knew the military offered me a better life and the opportunity to travel the world. When I told him that I was leaving for the military, I had already sworn in and was scheduled to leave in one week; needless to say, he cried like a baby, and I had never seen him since!

In April of 1980, I found myself in Fort Jackson, South Carolina, with temperatures of 103 degrees in the shade. The bus was filled with women from every walk of life. As we exited the bus, there were several drill sergeants yelling, "Welcome to the Army, you're no longer in control of your life! I will tell you when to sleep, eat, and go to the latrine (bathroom)!" This sounds like prison to me, I thought. Of course, I had already made my mind up that they could do what they wanted, I would do what I needed to be successful and finish the training. I got off the bus with a determination that I would not allow anyone or anything to break my spirit. I had a fighting determination not to quit or give up, which I was born with. As I look back, I have always been a fighter and one strong-minded to be successful at whatever I did. One of the first things they did was to separate us into groups (platoons) within the company and assign us a "battle buddy." A battle buddy is a partner assigned to a soldier in the US Army and other armed forces. The responsibilities of the battle buddy were to

1. Assist in and out of combat
2. Keep each other informed about current instructions, orders, and information
3. Encourage and increase morale
4. Improve safety and training in and out of combat
5. Improve communication and accountability
6. Build a community of peer support
7. Cover each other's back

Battle buddies operate together as a single unit (www.wearethemighty.com). Each soldier is responsible for preventing the other from becoming a casualty and holding them liable for their actions and whereabouts. This method of unity teaches teamwork, accountability, trust, and faith in your partner's ability to help keep you alive. Battle buddies in the kingdom of God are prayer partners, warriors, intercessors, ministers, and those whom we are connected in the body of Christ.

My prayer partner for twenty-three years, Anita, has become so connected that seldom times she would pray what I am seeing in the spirit. I remember years ago I had gotten laid off from my job, and she and I went to the unemployment office. When we got there, the entire place was packed. There was barely anywhere to sit. Both of us spotted a lady walk in and go straight to the bathroom. The lady looked a bit weathered. She looked at me and said, "Let's go to the bathroom!" We walked into the bathroom, and the lady said, "I just got hit by a car!" We began to pray for the lady, and blood started coming from her eyes and demons shooting from the top of her head. The lady explained that she was trying to get off of drugs and God sent her there! After we finished praying, I realized that I might have missed my name being called. When we walked out of the bathroom, the place was entirely empty, and the man called my name as we were walking out. We have witnessed the power of God so many times over these years as a result of our spiritual connection to God first and then to each other. We as believers must be so spiritually connected that we can pick up in the spirit when someone is in need of God's help! We must be first responders (quick to move, quick to obey, and quick to help). She is my battle (beauty) buddy, and we are built for battle.

 In basic training, each company had two drill sergeants in charge, who stayed in the barracks twenty-four hours a day. There were four platoons, and each had a new trainee platoon leader to be in charge. This leader was chosen as a result of military training prior to entry, such as ROTC or a program that allowed them to train with the Reserves or National Guard to get experience and receive rank. My battle buddy was Private Smith (Smithy), she was about four feet, and she came from the streets of Chicago. Smithy was not afraid of anything or anybody. Even though she was small in stature, she was large in confidence. Her walk and her talk displayed an attitude of confidence and gave off a spirit of "Don't you even try it!" The drill sergeants didn't even mess with Smithy. We both did everything together, and we became very close during boot camp.

Boot camp consisted of getting up around 4:00 a.m. daily for physical fitness. We were instructed to drink water, eat correctly, and get plenty of rest. Many mistakes are made on the battlefield because of sleep deprivation and fear. In order for us to be effective in a war (spiritually or naturally), we must first be in tip-top shape.

Physical Fitness versus Spiritual Fit

There are three phases to basic training:

1. Phase 1 (Red)

    - At arrival, the trainees get haircuts, uniforms, and are introduced to physical training and learning the core military values. I call this prep for the part!

2. Phase 2 (White)

    - During this phase, the trainees are introduced to tactical foot march, field training exercise, drill and ceremony, weaponry training, equipment skills, and situational training. Better spoken, prep work! When a chef is making a meal, they do what is called prep work!

3. Phase 3 (Blue)

    - This level involves intense weapons training (M16, grenade, riffle, AT4 (known as the Log)), field training exercises, and tactical foot march (10-15 kilometers, 6.21-9.32 miles).

Physical Fitness

Our training included running, road marches (wearing full Army gear in the sweltering heat), calisthenics, and weapons training. We ran six days a week while calling cadence (singing motivational sounds) to help everyone keep the rhythm. Many of the soldiers were falling out of formation during the runs and road marches. The entire company, which included men and women, had to turn around and get them. There were many lessons that we learned from this, such as teamwork and endurance, and we're only as strong as our weakest link. At the time, I really did not understand how all this had anything to do with war, but it was preparing us for battle. Preparation means to make ready beforehand. The US Army does not take a new recruit and sent them to the front line of battle before training them to fight. Since we are soldiers in the army of the Lord, we must be equipped for battle. Readiness is one thing, but being equipped is another. Being equipped is knowing what to do and how to do it effectively in order to prevent loss and gain the advantage of the enemy.

In the Military, there are several types of soldiers:

1. Reservist - trained and sent home to work, weekend training, and spent two weeks a year at summer camp. These are similar to Sunday morning churchgoers and maybe occasionally Wednesdays. Would you want this person in the Army, next to you in the foxhole?
2. National Guards - They are part of the reserve components of the United States Armed Forces; their motto, "Always Ready, Always There!"

3. Active Duty - full-time soldiers, always prepared for battle, looking for the enemy; they carry their weapons at all times. They are combat-ready leaders.
4. Special Forces - trained for special assignments or missions. In the kingdom, these are made up of chosen people with God-given special capabilities, which heed the call, pay the price, which may even consist of losing their lives.

As a soldier in the army of the Lord, there may be a time when someone may be weak in the Lord, and it is our responsibility to restore them into the fold and leave no one behind. One of my favorite movies is *We Were Soldiers* by Hal Moore and Joseph L. Galloway. The movie was released on February 25, 2002. Mel Gibson was the commander in chief and prayed for his enemies on a regular basis. On the day that they were going into war, he declared to his troops that "no one would be left behind." During the entire movie, he ensured his men that everyone would return to the family. He made good on his word, even though many returned injured, wounded, and in body bags. His concern for his troops was one of courage and commitment. As Christian, we must raise our love level up to reach those who are hurt and lost.

> *Brothers, if someone is caught in a trespass, you who are spiritual should restore him with a spirit of gentleness. But watch yourself, or you may be tempted.*
>
> —Galatians 6:1, New King James Version)

The word *restore*, in Greek, means to bring into proper condition (whether for the first time or after a lapse). Restoration is very important in the body of Christ. Many people are sitting in church hurt from the past, and no one is taking time to minister/disciple and restore them into the fold. The Lord told me that there are Christians who are spiritually hemorrhaging. We must not stand by, allowing the enemy of our souls to hinder our brothers and sisters in Christ. As the body of Christ, we must go to the hedges and highways and reach the lost, hurt, and broken. There are people in the pews who need help. Our discernment must be sharpened. Remember band-aids don't fix bullet holes, and we are our brother's keeper!

Spiritually Fit

In order to keep your spiritual muscles in shape and ready to "kick dragon and do battle," there are several essential elements that must be a part of your spiritual walk with God:

- ➤ Prayer, prayer, and more prayer - It can never be expressed enough how important prayer is to the kingdom of God for the believer.

    Praying always with all prayer and supplication in the spirit, and watching there unto with all perseverance and supplications for all saints.

    —*Ephesians 6:18, KJV*

In a natural war, the whole army is great, but in order for the ground troops to be more effective on the battlefield, there is something else they need. On a level battlefield, the visibility is limited; therefore, the ground troops need someone with an aboveground panoramic view who can see the big picture of the entire battlefield. They also need some type of communication device that will allow them to be in constant contact with the one with the aboveground view. In the military, we had radio operators, communication specialists, and aviation communicators. The radio operator is responsible for maintenance checks and service of equipment. The communications specialist handles public relations, information output, press releases and media requests, social media, and advertising efforts. The aviation communicator keeps the aircraft crew connected to the air and ground (www.Army.com). Prayer is important to keep our connection with God and those around us. It gives us a bird's eye view of what is going on in the spirit.

In spiritual warfare, for the believer, there is a command center. It is written, *"The Lord hath prepare his throne in heavens; and His kingdom ruleth over all" (Psalms 103:19, KJV). It is he that sitteth upon the circle of the earth and the inhabitants thereof are as grasshoppers, that stretcheth out the heavens as a curtain and spreadeth them out as a tent to dwell in (Isaiah 40:22, KJV).* God's throne is the command center of the universe. Prayer is the communication device used to contact the command center. The believers' reporting station is at a place called the Throne of Grace. *"Let us then approach the throne of grace with confidence, so that we may receive mercy and find grace to help us in our time of need" (Hebrew 4:16, KJV)* Our victory or defeat depends on our ability to keep in touch with the command center. Living life at ground level on the battlefield is no place for the kingdom believer (carnality). When we fight at ground level, we are at a terrible disadvantage, unprepared or unaware of pending enemy attacks. The Lord has the big picture in view and knows every planned attack and all things that are coming against us. *"And when Judas had taken the piece of bread, Satan entered into him. Then Jesus said to Judas, 'What you are about to do, do quickly'" (John 13:27, KJV).* When we are spiritually-minded, praying and hanging around the throne of grace and keeping in constant touch with the captain of our salvation, nothing will slip up on us. Constant communication with the command center will not deliver you from everything, but it will prepare you to go through with joy and victory. *"My brethren, count it all joy when ye fall into divers temptations; knowing this, that the trying of your faith worketh patience" (James 1:2, KJV).* Since prayer is vitally important, we will take a closer in depth look at prayer later.

CHAPTER TWO

The Dressing Room

To appoint unto them that mourn in Zion, to give unto them beauty for ashes, the oil of joy for mourning, the garment of praise for the spirit of heaviness; that they might be called trees of righteousness, the planting of the Lord, that he might be glorified.

—Isaiah 61:3, KJV

Before we can put on our armor, we must put on our garments or clothing. When I joined the Army, the first thing they did when we got off the bus was march us to the supply center. At the supply center, we were stripped of our civilian garments and given a uniform. Everyone had the same uniform, and there was no preference given to color or style, but we still maintained our individuality. God does not take away your uniqueness but works on our character. The uniform signified that we were now members of the same team. Any alterations to the uniform meant you were in division and subject to punishment. Our uniform consisted of a hat, shirt, pants, belt, and boots. This was a daily uniform, but our uniform for war was totally different. A camouflage uniform of defense (helmet, web gear, boots, weapons, and ammunition) was our war vestment. Before we received our weapon, we were taught the correct way to wear our uniform. Each item had to be cleaned, pressed, our boots shined, and the gib line aligned correctly (shirt, belt, and pants straight in a row).

Just like the kingdom of God, we must be dressed properly before we can engage in war. Before we talk about the armor of God, let's address the issue of what goes under the armor. The scripture talks about the garment of praise for the spirit of heaviness.

We all know that during spiritual warfare, it is sometimes hard to praise God when all hell is breaking loose. If we invite God in and allow praise to be our weapon, we saturate our surroundings and the spirit of heaviness is disarmed. When we put on the garment of praise, we wrap ourselves in the presence of God. Have you ever felt heavy but just began to sing praises to God and the spirit of heaviness lifted? The garment of praise is not only a weapon, but also a covering and a veil. Jehoshaphat appointed singers (worship team) to go before the army, and the Lord set an ambush against the Ammonites and Moabites at Mount Seir, which caused the enemy to fight one against another. When we praise God, that confuses the enemy. To believe in the Lord Jesus Christ is referred to as putting him on as a garment.

> *I will rejoice greatly in the Lord, my soul will exult in my God, for He has clothed me with garments of salvation and wrapped me in a robe of righteousness, as a groom wears a priestly headdress and as a bride adorns herself with her jewels.*
>
> —Isaiah 61:10, KJV

> *I will sing for joy in God, explode in praise from deep in my soul! He dressed me up in a suit of Salvation, he outfitted me in a robe of righteousness, as a bridegroom who puts on a tuxedo and a bride a jeweled tiara.*
>
> —*Isaiah 61:10, The Message Bible*

What is a garment? The Hebrew meaning for garment is to wrap, to cover, to veil, or to clothe.

Let's Put on the Whole Armor of God!

> *Put on the whole armor of God, that ye may be able to stand against the wiles of the devil.*
>
> —*Ephesians 6:11, KJV*

> *Wherefore, take unto you the whole armor of God, that ye may be able to withstand in the evil day, having done all to stand.*
>
> —*Ephesians 6:13, KJV*

The word does not say anything about running from the devil or putting armor on our back. Armor means a weapon or offensive tool used for war. The fact that Paul mentioned the whole armor of God twice in the same chapter shows us the importance of the whole armor and not part of the armor. We cannot pick and choose our armor, but we must be completely armed for battle. Let's look at Ephesians 6:14:

> *Stand therefore, having your loins girt about with truth, and having on the breastplate of righteousness . . .*

This scripture depicts the armor of a Roman soldier equipped in full battle dress. In the military, the importance of wearing the uniform was stressed because difference indicated division and out of order. If my uniform was different, then my fellow battle buddies may mistake me for an intruder. In the kingdom, we must never take off our web gear (armor); we must sleep in it.

The Shield of Faith

The shield is used to protect, to defend, to cover, to conceal, and to ward off the fiery darts of the enemy. The devil is shooting fiery darts at us, and often those darts take the form of lies, negative suggestions, and mind-controlling thoughts. When people lie about us, their words are like darts aimed at our hearts. We must turn them away by holding up the shield of faith. Faith is the confidence in the testimony of another. Jesus's life was a testimony to all believers.

> *Now faith is the substance of things hoped for, the evidence of things not seen.*
>
> *—Hebrews 11:1, KJV)*

> *Without faith it is impossible to please God, because anyone who approaches Him must believe that He exists and that He rewards those who earnestly seek Him.*
>
> *—Hebrews 11:6, KJV*

The opposite of faith is not doubt; it is fear. Anything that is not of faith is sin. Even with the threat of war, we must not fear the one who can kill the body, but we must fear the one who can kill the body and soul (Matthew 10:28, KJV). The word of God is a shield; it is our protection and weapon against the enemy.

Cover Your Head (Helmet of Salvation)

The helmet is used to cover your head, which is the seat of your mind. *Philippians 2:5 says, "Let this mind be in you, that is also in Christ Jesus."* There have been many sermons preached on deliverance of the mind and positive thinking. In order to get and keep our minds delivered, it takes action on our part. There are several things that we must do. We must

1. Hear and heed the message that is being preached—faith comes by hearing the word of God.
2. Study to show ourselves approved.
3. Begin to apply the word to our lives. "Hearing is one thing, but listening is an entirely different level!"
4. Protect our minds and ears (gates) by watching what we look at, listen to, and even speak of.

After we have done these things, we can begin to do what *Philippians 4:8, KJV* says, *"Think on those things, that are true, honest, just, pure and lovely and of a good report."* We must renew our minds with the word of God. *Renew* means to renovate and/or reform. We must allow the word of God to renovate our minds, and some of us need home improvement. One of my favorite shows is *Fixer Upper*. In this show, a couple helps a person select a house in a desired neighborhood. The house is usually old, outdated, and sometimes in disrepair. After many hours of labor and a set budget, the couple takes the house and transforms it into something unrecognizable and beautiful to the homeowners. This is how the word of God is designed: to change us into his image and likeness from the inside out.

If we do not protect our minds, the enemy will have us thinking ungodly thoughts. When we allow the enemy to deposit negative thoughts in our minds and we do not reject it with the word of God, it gets deposited into our spirits and causing us to sin. Sin starts in our mind first. So many Christians are living defeated lives because we are not taking the time to renew our minds. One day without prayer makes one weak. It is not enough to attend church once a week and expect to be a strong Christian. This is like a soldier training for war once a week and expecting to wipe out the enemy. Imagine if we only ate once a week; we would be so weak, we could barely walk.

Double-mindedness is also a problem in the church. Many saints speak one thing and believe another. Scripture does not only change your heart, but it must also be accompanied by faith and application of the word. James 1:8, KJV puts it this way: *"A double minded man is unstable (unreliable) in all his ways.* Double-minded can also mean two-faced. We must cast down imaginations. *Our imaginations can take us in places we dare not go; therefore, we must cast down every imagination and every high thing that exalted itself against the knowledge of God and bring every thought to the obedience of Christ (2 Corinthians 10:5, KJV).* We must pull down strongholds. How do I pull down strongholds? You must apply spiritual pressure in prayer, using spiritual weapons (prayer, praise, and worship). Jesus, in Luke 4, when he was led in the wilderness by the Holy Ghost to be tempted by the devil, he applied pressure by putting the word on it. You must have an "it is written" for every "if thou be!" The word of God must match the situation or warfare that you are currently facing. Many Christians are defeated because they are bringing a knife to a gunfight. The only thing that moves the enemy is the word of God!

Slay That Devil (The Sword of the Spirit)

The sword of the spirit is the only defensive weapon that is given to the believer. The sword is described as a knife, dirk (which is a dagger) used for war or judicial punishment. A dagger is a short pointed weapon with sharp edges. All other pieces of armor are for the body, but the sword is being used as weapon. There are many different types of conventional weapons used in an earthly war. In addition, the Bible does speak of various weapons, praise, worship, and many others, which we will explore later. *Hebrews 4:12 says that the word is sharper than a two-edged sword.* We must take the sword of the spirit and use it to back the devil up. Jesus used the word on the devil. He used the word against the enemy, rebuking the devil and causing him to flee. If he had to use the word, "How much more should we?" When we exercise the word on the devil, we declare war against him and his demons. *Submit to God and resist the devil, and he will flee from you (James 4:7).* How do I resist the devil? Resist with the word. The Greek meaning for *resist* is to set against, withstand, and oppose. *When the enemy comes in like a flood, the spirit of the Lord will raise a standard against him (Isaiah 59:19).* No word, no resistance, no victory!

Strap Up (The Belt of Truth)

The belt was a wide leather strap that went around the waist, not to hold the pants, but was used to protect the loins. Loins are portion of the back, one of the weakest and most sensitive parts of the body. One strong blow to this area can break the spine and leave you paralyzed. To have your loins girded about with truth means to have the weakest part protected with the truth of the word. If you pay close attention to the armor, you will notice that the back is uncovered. Like my late spiritual apostle mother used to say, "Never turn your back on the enemy!" When your back is turned, you are either walking away, running away, or your guard is down.

Each one of us has weak areas in our personal lives that we must keep covered in prayer and under the blood. Identifying this area is extremely important because this is where the devil tries to gain access. During the weak moments and times of our lives, Satan attacks the hardest. God's strength is made perfect in my weakness (2 Corinthians 12:9, KJV). When he attacks us with his lies, we must counterattack with the truth of the word. If Satan can convince us that he is telling the truth, he will begin to deactivate your faith. The importance of studying the word cannot be stressed enough because if you don't know the truth, you will believe a lie.

Guard Your Heart (The Breastplate of Righteous)

The breastplate is used to cover the breast and chest area, which includes several vital organs, such as the lungs and heart. Righteousness means to be in right standing with God. It is in our hearts were the word of God must be kept. The heart is the seat of our emotions; out of it comes our sense of self-worth. Many times what you are or are not came from what someone has done or spoken that entered into your heart and began to produce fruit. David said, "Write your word upon the tables of my heart so that I might not sin against you. Our heart is one of the most important organs in our body. *Proverbs 4:23, KJV says, "Out of the heart flows the issues of life."* What we fill our hearts with will come out of our mouth, especially when pressure is applied. Righteousness is absolute faith in and commitment to God (Romans 4:5, KJV). When we received Jesus Christ as Savior, Master, and King, we became righteous. Our righteousness is of God and not of ourselves.

Feet Shod (Gospel of Peace)

To shod means to bind to one's feet; put on shoes or sandals. Proper shoes are critical for protection from pain that could cripple the entire body. Ladies, when your feet hurt, your entire body hurts, and sometimes comfort rules over cuteness. Nothing can give your feet a firmer stance than to be fully dependent upon the unshakable, incorruptible and unchangeable word of God. Ever bought a pair of shoes that fit good in the store, only to find out later that they were only good for looks? One of the most important elements of a soldier's battle gear are the boots. The boots protect from the elements and the danger of stepping on snakes, spiders, and poisonous reptiles, insects and animals.

The gospel is the good news—good news about the death, burial, and resurrection of our Lord and Savior Jesus Christ. As sons and daughter of God, we must live our life as a witness to sinners and be prepared to share the gospel, the good news, everywhere we go. Look at every opportunity as an assignment from God. We have been commissioned by God to share the gospel and go to the hedges and highway and compel men to come to him. *Colossians 1:13, KJV says we must remember that we were translated from the power of darkness unto the kingdom of God.*

CHAPTER THREE

Zeroing Your Weapon

For the weapons of our warfare, are not carnal, but mighty through God to the pulling down of strong holds.

—*2 Corinthians 10:4, KJV*

After several weeks of basic training, we were introduced to weapons training. We were assigned our M16 weapon and taught how to clean and take it apart. The gun range had strict rules to keep the weapon down range and always assume that it is always loaded. There are three level of weapons qualification course in the military, which included marksman, sharpshooter, and expert. There are techniques to shooting your weapon called grouping and zeroing. Zeroing the weapon meant to personalize, adjust your scope in order to make it easier to hit the target. Grouping is considered hitting the target within a certain ratio of each other. This meant that you would be able to shoot the enemy. The requirement was to hit a certain number of targets, which would qualify you to graduate and move to the next level. A marksman is one who is skilled in precision shooting and must hit twenty-three to twenty-nine out forty targets to obtain this level. A sharpshooter must qualify by hitting thirty to thirty-five targets. Last, an expert badge is earned by hitting thirty-six to forty of the targets (www.military.com). If you did not qualify your weapon, you had to wear a steel pot with cherries painted all over it, and everyone in the battalion would know that you "bow-lowed," which meant you could not shoot. Needless to say, I believe that was one of the times that I prayed the hardest doing training and God answered. I was overjoyed that I did not have to wear that ridiculous helmet—a badge of shame and dishonor. Many trainees were recycled because they simply could not qualify. Many Christians are spiritually stagnated or plain old stuck in religion because they refuse to take the time to learn their spiritual weapons. This is one of the reasons why we see the enemy running amok in the church and the world!

There are conventional and nonconventional weapons. Conventional weapons are ordinary and customary. A nonconventional weapon is not ordinary. In the Old Testament days, the children of Israel fought a physical enemy. Many times God would manifest his power in a tangible way. *The children of Israel did not have the indwelling spirit of God (Holy Ghost) living in them (Acts 2:4, Roman 8:11), but they had the over shadowing (presence of God).* There were times when God would manifest himself in a visible way through nature, animals, other people, and many other ways. In addition, God would allow his people or man of God to see in the spirit and speak to him face-to-face. Since Jesus gave his life as a ransom, we now fight a spiritual enemy. If we are going to remain victorious, we must know our weapons and how to effectively engage the adversary. Before we explore conventional weapons, we will take a look at nonconventional weapons:

- Voice of God - When God speaks, things, situations, and atmospheres change. In *Psalms 29, the Bible declares that the voice of the Lord shaketh the wilderness. It was his voice that separated the sand from the sea. It was his voice that said, "Let there be light," and so it was (Genesis 1:3, KJV)*. God called each and every one us out of darkness (our decision, but his voice). God speaks to our hearts, minds, and spirits through the power of the spoken word. If God spoke from heaven now, most of us would be frightened. Just like the voice of God, our words have creative power. The power of life and death is in the tongue. *Psalms 45:1, KJV says your tongue is the pen of a skillful or ready writer.* We will devote an entire chapter to exploring the power of the tongue.
- Shout/Trumpet - *On the seventh day, they walked around the city seven times (the number of completion), and the people shouted when the priest blew the trumpet and the wall fell flat (Joshua 6:1-20, KJV)*. The word *shout*, in Hebrew, means a battle cry, raised a war cry, sound an alarm, and to shout for joy. This wall, about six feet, fourteen feet thick, was used by the guards to walk around and guard the city of Jericho. No one was allowed to go in or out; it was sealed shut. The walls stood between them, and the victory that God declared belonged to them. God used the trumpet and the shout to bring down the wall. Their voice activated something in the spirit that caused a natural reaction. A shout can bring down the walls of depression, oppression, discouragement, stress, and frustration. The trumpet was an alarm to declare war on the enemy. Your shout can declare war in the heavenlies.
- Praise - Jehoshaphat appointed singers to sing praises to the Lord as they went out before the army and to say, "Praise the

Lord for his mercy endureth forever, and when they began to sing praises, the Lord set an ambush against the children of Ammon." Have you ever had an enemy on your job who brought confusion and you declared in your spirit that "today the enemy will not disturb my peace" and you began to lift up the name of Jesus? The peace of God came in and overshadowed the job to the point the enemy was speechless. God set an ambush against the enemy using your praises *(2 Chronicles 20:22, KJV)*. Our praise can release a spiritual attack on the enemy and catch him off guard. An ambush is a surprise attack from concealed position.

- His Strong and Outstretched Arm - When we pray, God flexes his muscles. We are asking God for his strength, his saving power, his delivering power, and we lean and depend on his outstretched arms to wage war on the enemy. *In Luke 1:21, as Mary waited for the birth of Jesus, Elizabeth confessed that in bringing Jesus, God showed "strength with his arm"; this was God flexing his muscles.*

- God's Angelic Intervention - *Elisha prays that God would open the servant's eyes, that he may see in the spirit realm that the angels, chariots and horses of the Lord out the number the enemy (2 Kings 6:16-17).* Even though the enemy could not see the angels, the divine intervention of the Lord was present. We each have angels assigned to us. *For He gives his angels charge over thee to watch over thee in all our ways (Psalm 91:11, KJV).*

I remember my daughter who was nine years old at the time. We were traveling at night from a family conference located in Austell, Georgia. We heard a sound from the outside of the car and realized that something was wrong with the tire. The distance home was about an hour drive. I began to pray. It was dark, and we were about to pass a dangerous area. As we traveled, my daughter began to sing praise and worship songs. This area was on Highway 285 where eighteen-wheelers come around a very sharp curve; needless to say, this was where the tire went completely flat. I stopped the car and started to get out. My daughter yelled, "Oh no, Mom, please don't get out!" I looked in the rearview mirror and saw a thirty-foot angel standing under the bridge where the sharp curve was located. I said, "Lord, thank you for the angel of protection," and my daughter said, "I saw it too but thought it was a demon!" This was my first time seeing an angel but not my last.

- Weapon of Love - The power of the love of God can disarm the devil and break every chain. Love held Jesus to the cross, his love for you and me. During my twenty-four years of marriage, I prayed faithfully for the salvation of my husband for twenty-one years, but it was the love of God that drew him, and love allowed me hold on to the promise of salvation. I knew that God would save him, but I just did not know when. Needless to say, he got saved three days before he died. I want to take this time to encourage a wife or young couple who may feel like throwing in the towel on their marriage. Marriage is not for punks or people who don't like to fight and cover their mate. God can and will fix it. You just have to hold on and pray. You must trust God that he is working something out in you and your spouse as well. Remember he sees the bigger picture! *It is only a test!* The teacher is always silent during a test.

I remember when I was in the military, I visited Paris, and during my trip, we took a tour to a glass-making plant (factory). The glass started out as liquid sand and reached temperatures of 3,090 degrees Fahrenheit. The glassmaker, wearing protective gloves, took the lump of molten glass and wrapped it around a long open pipe and slowly rotated the pipe. He blew air through the pipe, and the glass shaped up into a balloon. After he got it to the desired size, he began to shape it. It was a dangerous and long process, but the outcome was beautiful. It took a lot of time, skill, and patience to deliver such a beautiful vessel. The process that you may be going through may be hard, but in the end, a beautiful testimony is going to come out of it. Trust God during the process!

> *Love takes no pleasure in evil, but rejoices in truth. It bears all things, believes all things, hopes all things, endures all things.*
>
> *—1 Corinthians 13:6-7*

Love does what no weapon on the face of this earth can do. Love gives us the power to hold on through a situation that looks hopeless. Love don't change—people do! I just want to encourage you to don't give up on that unsaved loved one. I am a living witness that God specializes in hard cases. Hold on, help is on the way! Utilize your weapon of love!

Nonconventional Weapons - Nature as a Weapon

All throughout the Bible, God used nature as a force to fight the enemy for the children of Israel. God caused the Red Sea to part when Moses stretched forth the rod and the east wind parted the sea *(Exodus 14:21, KJV)*. God used an ordinary walking stick to become the defense and way out for his children. In *Joshua 10:9-10,* five kings of Amorites came against Gibeonites to make war, and he calls for Joshua's assistance. The Lord told Joshua "to fear not, for I have delivered them into your hands." The Lord sent hailstones from heaven upon them, and the enemy flee. There were more people who died from the hailstone than in the war.

Lethal Weapon
The Blood of Jesus

For even the Son of Man did not come to be served, but to serve and to give His life as a ransom for many.

—Mark 10:45

The next day John saw Jesus coming toward him and said, "Look, the Lamb of God, who takes away the sin of the world!"

—John 1:29

The blood of Jesus is the central power of our entire redemption. The blood covers sin on God's side and removes it on man's side. The blood restored what sin destroyed. The blood is God's way of dealing with sin or sinners. Sacrificial blood always meant the offering of a life. What the blood of bulls and goats could not do, there is a more excellent sacrifice, and that was the blood of Jesus. The Lord Jesus did not sacrifice his life to spare us from sacrificing ours. Rather, he did it to make the sacrifice of our lives possible and desirable. We give ourselves and lives as to press into the full power of the new life, which was provided by the blood. We must separate ourselves from sin and carnality and self-will. The power of the blood operates in our lives without hinderance, if we have a yielded vessel.

We will review a few things that the blood does with a surrendered soul:

1. Reconciliation through the Blood. It puts man back in fellowship with God. *Reconciliation* means making peace after an engagement of war or readmission to the presence and favor of a person after rebellion against the person. In other words, "atonement" (at one) with God *(Romans 5:11, KJV)*.

   Sin was viewed as a breach of covenant (contract) between God and man. Sin brought a distance between God and the children of Israel, and so it is with us. The day of atonement was designed as the day when unintentional sins of people could be forgiven. Deliberate sins were forgiven only by prayer and repentance *(Leviticus 16:1-31, KJV)*.

2. Cleansing by the Blood - *Cleansing* means to remove all stains of guilt and shame. Mankind's fall made sin a generational issue *(Genesis 3:1-19, KJV)*. The blood of Jesus cleanses us from all sins *(1 John 1:7, KJV)*.

3. Sanctification through the Blood of Jesus. *Sanctification* means the process of being holy, resulting in a change of lifestyle for the believer, consecration and holiness. Since God exists in the realm of the spirit (holy) rather than the profane, all that pertains to him must come into his presence holy.

4. Union through the Blood. *Union* or *unity* means being undivided and in oneness with God. Jesus encouraged the disciples to experience unity with God *(John 17:11, KJV)*.

5. Victory over Satan through the Blood of Jesus. *Victory* means overcoming, conquering, and subduing the enemy. Thanks be unto God who has given us victory through our Lord and Savior Jesus Christ *(Romans 7:25, KJV)*.

CHAPTER FOUR

Armed and Dangerous

For the word of God is quick, and powerful, and sharper than any two edge sword, piercing even to dividing asunder of soul and spirit, and of the joints and marrow, and is a discerner of the thoughts and intents of the heart.

—Hebrews 4:12

A friend and I decided to go to the Sports Academy. We both were women veterans and familiar with handling a weapon. We located the sign that said "ammo." I approached the counter and was greeted by a young man, asking to assist us. I requested to see a .380 handgun! As we were looking at the weapon, two Caucasian men walked up behind us. One man proceeded to say, "I am retired military and a retired police officer. Why do you want to purchase a weapon?" I replied, "For protection!" With a smile on his face, he began to explain the different types of guns on display that he thought would be a good fit. I explained to him that I had a 9mm, but it was too heavy to carry in my purse and did not have a safety on it. He suggested a revolver. I said, "Why, a revolver?" He explained that most times, if something happens, you may forget to take the safety off. "A revolver will only shoot if you 'pull the trigger'!"

Customized Weapon

When I got home, the Lord began to say, "There are many weapons. *Use your customized weapon,* the one that is designed for your situation and circumstances that you can aim at the enemy and take him out." The word *customized* means to be modified to suit a particular individual or task (www.dictionary.com).

Our prayer must be customized to fit our situations and circumstances in order to be effective in this spiritual fight. Customizing your weapon must start with studying the scripture, where your life is currently located. I often tell people, "Don't study in Genesis if your life is in Revelations!" Now what does this really mean? If you are currently facing a situation and feel there is no way out, look up the word concerning your situation and customize your weapon and put the word on your situation. A customized prayer life is a powerful life. David understood this principle very well when he told Saul that he could not use his armor to go to war. His personal involvement working with the sheep in the field equipped him to fight the giant on the hill. David worked in the pasture but was being prepped by God to become a king and modern-day pastor.

"Then Saul clothed David in his own tunic, put a bronze helmet on his head, and dressed him in armor. David strapped his sword over the tunic and tried to walk, but he was not accustomed to them. 'I cannot walk in these,' David said to Saul. 'I am not accustomed to them.' So, David took them off" (1 Samuel 17:39, KJV). Even though David valued the

opinion and suggestion of Saul, it wasn't until he tried it on and realized, "This may have worked for Saul, but is will not work for me! It might be your size but, not your fit! One size does not fit all during war! Being familiar with the anointing on your life and how God uses you will ensure that your weapon stays loaded and that you are armed for the battle. We can no longer make it on the prayers of our ancestors. You must have a personal relationship with our Savior and Master. Prayer will work, if you work it!

I have never really been one to walk in fear, when it concerned my safety, until I got older and the enemy reminded me of how my father died. I was between the age of five and six years old when my father was walking home from his business and was attacked by several men and robbed. It was in below-zero weather, and his body was found in an abandoned house several days later. My mother never really told us the entire story but gave us enough information to determine that he was murdered and robbed at a young age. As I drew closer to God, this fear lifted. We must really be careful what we allow the enemy to torment us with. The devil will try to weaponize our shortcomings and past hurts to disarm our purpose in God. Thank God, David did not allow his past rejection from his father and family to hinder the kingship anointing on his life. God was training him on the back side of the mountain. I often wondered, "Where was David's mother, and why didn't she speak up for him?" There was a "But God" working on David's behalf; this situation was customizing his weapons. David's ability to handle the lion and bear showed that God was teaching him hand-to-hand combat and giving him strategic methods of taking the enemy down and out. Every situation we go through is designed to equip us to fight the next-level devil. The lion and the bear were just training grounds for what real enemies David would face later.

Concealed Weapon

Several years ago, I was led to get a concealed weapon license. Georgia has a Castle Doctrine, which is the stand your ground and pertains to your property, home and car, and workspace. The law entails the fact each individual has the right to be safe and secure within his or her own home or castle (www.usconcealedcarry.com). As believers, we must stand flatfoot and bold and declare to enemy that he will not destroy or take over our families. When we plead the blood of Jesus over our lives, we conceal ourselves with the blood of Jesus. The blood of Jesus still works—it never loses its power.

Secret Weapon

One of the most powerful weapons is the evidence of tongues and the Holy Ghost. *"For he who speaks in a tongue does not speak to men, but to God. Indeed, no one understands him, he utters mysteries in the Spirit (1 Corinthians 14:2, KJV).* It is like a Morse Code in the spirit. It gives us the ability to speak to God, and the enemy does not have a clue what we are talking about. The International Morse Code was the method that was used during wartime to communicate with dots and dashes so that the enemy would not be able to understand the message. It was utilized mainly in the shipping industry for the safety of the ships. This type of communication was used during World War 2, Korean and Vietnam Wars (www.britannica.com).

During Harriet Tubman times, they used slave songs to express their struggle for freedom, and many of the songs were coded with directions and instructions on how to escape. These songs gave details, called signal songs, which gave maps and information about where to meet (www.harriet-tuman.org). This was a clever method because many slaves could not read or write. Speaking in tongues has a similar effect because it gives the ability to move under the Holy Ghost radar. As I observed the movie, it was apparent that Harriet Tubman was being directed by the Holy Ghost. She was able to move without being detected by the enemy; as a result, many lives were set free. I am determined that if we move under the unction of the Holy Ghost, many souls will be saved and set free.

CHAPTER FIVE

Demonaic Rank and Orders

For we wrestle not against flesh and blood, but against principalities, against powers, against, the rulers of the darkness of this world; against spiritual wickedness in high places

—*Ephesians 6:12, KJV*

What is the meaning of *rank*? Rank is military order or row, a line of soldiers standing side by side in close order, also used for determining your status in the military. Rank during wartime and peace are different in nature. During wartime, it is a lot easier to get promoted for those that show leadership qualities and the ability to follow orders to the letter. In addition, if a position needs to be filled as a result of death or injury of another soldier, then one can be promoted. Promotions are not always based on who has seniority. Peacetime has different guidelines for promotions, which include testing, time in service, job performance, ability to follow orders, and leadership abilities.

Spiritual promotions are a combination of a lot of things; it is never based on anyone else (promotions come from above). They are much like peacetime and are based on trials, obedience, faith, and endurance, just to name a few. Your natural age or how long you have been saved has little to do with your spiritual rank. Your relationship with God and your obedience plays a significance part in your spiritual development. Just as a relationship with a friend develops, it is built on communication, trust, faith, and time. The more you learn about God, the more your faith grows. Getting to know God and spending time with him is vital.

Before we can go to battle, we must first understand Satan's strategy, method, and spiritual authority. One of my favorite sports is boxing. The fight between Evander Holyfield and Mike Tyson took an interesting spin when Tyson bit Holyfield on the ear (www.thegruelingtruth.com). This shows a spiritual element that when the enemy feels like he is losing, he will try to do something that will catch us off-guard and make us forfeit the fight. Before the boxing match ever begins, the opponent spends countless hours watching tapes, studying the skills, abilities, and weak points of the other fighter. In order for us to maintain victory, we must study our opponent (Satan). Now we are going to take a look at the similarities to Satan's army and the US Army.

Satan's Army

Principalities are headship, dominion, chief rulers. These are demons that give orders to powers. Powers are forces, delegated influence, capacity, authority, and jurisdiction. They receive instructions from principalities. Rulers of darkness of this world are called *kosmokrator*. A *kosmokrator* is Greek for world ruler, in charge of corruption and harm. Darkness means obscurity, dark and blind. Spiritual wickedness means iniquities, plots, sins, malice, hurtful, evil, mischief, guilt, and grievous. These are little demons that we come in contact with on a daily basis in our homes and places of business. High places translate to the place where they abode, dwell, stay, tarry as "heavenly place," which can include the sanctuaries of churches. In a nutshell, orders are given by principalities to powers to carry out an assignment and is influenced by rulers of darkness of this world and spiritual wickedness in heavenly places. The Bible says that Satan is the prince of the power of the air (Ephesian 2:2, KJV, *Holman Bible Dictionary*).

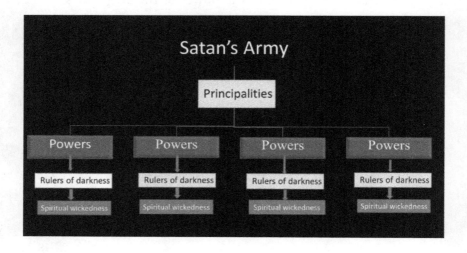

Satan's Weapons

One of the most dominant elements the enemy uses against the believer is fear. Fear is false evidence appearing real. It is believed that most things we worry about do not occur. *God has not given us the spirit of fear, but of power love and sound mind (2 Timothy 1:7, KJV).* Fear is used to alter our faith and cause us to walk into doubt and unbelief. Doubt and unbelief are enemies of our soul because we must walk by faith and not by sight. I am a firm believer that if the enemy can move us from a place of faith, he has got us right where he wants us.

Division is another weapon the enemy used against the church as a whole. It causes believers to come against one another instead of unifying in the fight. Some victories must be won corporately and not individually. The Bible says that after Cain had murdered his brother as a result of envy and jealousy, he responded to God's question of his whereabouts with *"I know not; am I my brother's keeper?" (Genesis 4:9, KJV)* This very element of disrespect and dishonor for his brother's life shows the value he placed on stuff more than his own blood. The world we live in has released a spirit of materialism and people's life has little to no value!

One of my favorite stories in the Bible is the story of David and Saul. Saul was chosen by the people, but David was ordained and anointed by God. The division in the kingdom erupted when Saul became jealous of David's victories being song by the women. This is a great example of competition and comparison that we often see in church, where people are competing over positions and titles. The enemy loves this type of fight because he just stands back and watch the believers destroy the plan of God and one another without his help. In order to deactivate this type of foolishness, we must focus on our God-given assignment and wait for your gift to make room for you. Truth be told, there is enough work to be done in the kingdom without fighting over who should be doing what. In addition, if you take a look around, there are more sinners than saints, and we have our work cut out for us. Only you can work your garden, or as my apostle says, "Work your cave!" As I often say, "Stay in your lane before you get ran over!"

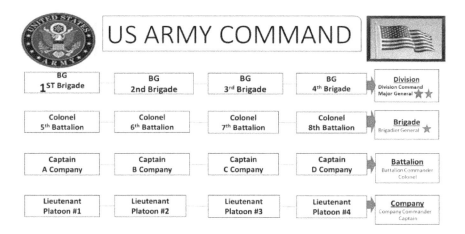

US Army Rank and Order

The US Army troops are divided into progressively larger groups, each led by officer of higher rank. To make it simple, we will begin with the bottom of the chain of command and work our way up. A platoon of men is led by a platoon commander, usually a lieutenant. A lieutenant is a junior commissioned officer, which can be earned several ways: by attending the military academy, army reserves officers training, officer candidate school, or direct appointment. Four platoons make up a company, which is led by a company commander, which is usually a captain. A captain is a commissioned officer promoted from a first lieutenant. Four companies are grouped together to form a battalion, under the leadership of a battalion commander, which is led by a colonel. A colonel is the senior field officer-grade commissioned officer. Four battalions form a brigade under the command of a brigadier general. Four brigades make up a division, under the authority of a division commander, a higher rank general, and so on up the scale. The hierarchy of officers make up what is called the chain of command, which reaches all the way from the platoon level to the president of the United States who serves as the commander in chief of all US Armed Forces (www.Army.com).

In addition, there are different types of combat arms, such as cavalry, infantry, artillery, and air assault that serve within the military, which make up the armed forces. In times past, the cavalry was made up of horsemen. They rode on horses and engage, fought, and defeat the enemy. The infantry were foot soldiers that fought hand-to-hand combat. The artillery soldiers were responsible for surveillance, target acquisition, and indirect fire to engage the enemy. Air assault was made up of helicopter operations, rappelling, sling load (which hook heavy equipment) (www.stripes.com). As believers, we must know our spiritual position and stand in the gap. If the military can organize a powerful force, then why not the saints? Each have different methods, tactics, and training to develop their soldiers, but all are clear on their mission and assignment. There are many different branches of service, but they all work together to keep our country safe.

Comparing – Demoniac and Natural Order

Satan's army has rank and order, with each demon having responsibilities and assignments that they carry out every day. Every demon is clear on their assignments, and there is no cross-pollinating or competing for positions or status. We as Christians must be clear of our purpose and know our *metron* (assignment).

In the US Army, each soldier is given an assignment and the duty to assist other soldiers to complete the job at any cost. In order to accomplish this, there must be unity and harmony, and everyone must follow orders from their chain of command. The church must shift our mindset and become kingdom-oriented. It is time out for church as usual. You may hear me say this more than once, but the next highest level of casualties that come from war is from friendly fire. We must stop the Christian killing within the church. Stop using our mouth to curse one another and get on our knees and pray until deliverance comes. One prayer that Jesus prayed, which has yet to be answered, "Lord, make us one!" The poison of the church is the spirit of offense, jealousy, and division. These subjects cannot be taught enough. We must stop putting band aids on bullet holes and shut these spirits down in the spirit realm, and sometimes these people must be confronted in the spirit of love. I have seen these spirits destroy churches, business, families, and friendships. These three spirits work hand and hand to divide and conquer, leaving wounded, injured, and broken warriors on the battlefield. If we ever get together as a body of Christ, the kingdom of hell will be in serious trouble.

CHAPTER SIX

Shut Your Trap and Open Your Mouth

Thou art snared with the words of thy own mouth; thou are taken with the words of thy mouth.

—Proverbs 6:2)

From the fruit of his mouth a man's belly is filled; with the harvest from his lips he is satisfied. Life and death are in the power of the tongue, and those who love it will eat fruit.

—Proverbs 18:20-21, KJV

Words as Weapons

The word *snare*, in Hebrew, means a trap or to lay bait. One of my favorite scenes in the movie *Titanic* (James Cameron, 1997) is when one of the crewmen has loaded people on the rescue ship and one of the passengers began to demand that he go back because the boats was not full. He yells at her and says, "Shut that whole in your face, or their will be another empty seat on this boat!" He further explains to her that there were a limited number of seats remaining, and if they went back, the other passengers would drown them all in a desperate need to save themselves. The veracity of the words spoken by the passenger was accurate and the right thing to do, but the outcome would have been more costly than the attempt to rescue others. We must think about the results of words spoken by us and to us over our circumstances, situations, and families. I remember, as a child, you could talk about anybody, but my mother, those where fighting words. This same kind of fight must break out against the kingdom of darkness. I never really understood how we could be fighters in the world but come into the kingdom of God and punk out! Could it be that we do not know who we are, so we fail to exercise kingdom authority? David was a warrior and winner before ever becoming king. His training did not start on the battlefield with men. I am a firm believer that what you do in private with God shows publicly.

Our mouth is a trap (bait) and can release words of hurt, bitterness, offense, and discouragement. One of our greatest defensive weapons against a public attack is silence and prayer. I have learned, over the years, that some things do not need to be glorified with an answer! Public attack, private prayers always counter the attack of the enemy. You can do more damage on your knees with your trap shut but your mouth open. Think about it: A trap is designed to catch an animal or someone off-guard and restrict their moment. When we allow negative words to be released into the atmosphere, you have just released a trap for Satan to use against you or others. Don't give the enemy a loaded gun! There are times when Satan takes those words and creates a situation. Have God ever told you to "shut up"?

As children of God, we must be very careful what we release out of our mouth. Our words have creative power, both negative and positive. Doctors will tell you when a person is in a coma, the last thing to go is the hearing. Many times, when they are giving medical updates to the family, they will request you to step out of the room so that the patient cannot hear. When my late husband had become terminally ill, the doctor pulled me out of the room and said, "We have done all we can do!"

There are times when things have been spoken to me, and it did not agree with my spirit, by people of faith, doctors, and even family. I would boldly and clearly say "I don't receive that!" Stop agreeing with the adversary of our souls. If the devil is bold enough to say it out loud, we must be bold enough to rebuke him out loud. Stand your ground and don't take down! Don't allow words to cause your faith to waiver.

Church Weapons

Demoniac grenades are weapons used within the church, weapons of slaughter, gossip, jealously, envy, competing and comparing for positions and titles, backstabbing and backbiting. A backbiter is a backstabber who has simply misplaced their knife. A grenade is a military weapon that is shaped like a lemon or lime with a pin at the top (www.madehow.com and www.dictionary.com). It is thrown when the enemy is within close range. Once the pin is removed, you have about thirty seconds to throw it and run to safety. Many Christians, or should I say believers in the body of Christ, are allowing themselves to be used by the enemy to do demolition and destruction to the church by way of mouth. My spiritual godmother would say, "Don't put your mouth on people because you do not know who holds the key to your deliverance!" The mouth is a powerful weapon that we allow the enemy to infiltrate the church with gossip and rumors.

The Bible states, *"Set me as a seal upon your heart, as a seal upon thine arm; for love is as strong as death; jealously is cruel as the grave . . ." (Song of Solomon 8:6, KJV)* I never clearly understood that until I read the story of Cain and Abel. Cain killed Abel because he was full of jealously and envy. I call this *friendly fire*. On the same team serving the same God and fighting the same opposing forces, yet Cain kills Abel. Why would you kill your help? You have now reduced your fighting force by one, and there is a spiritual gap. Sounds more like church against kingdom. This happens when we do not understand who the real enemy is, the accuser of the brother, that old serpent, the adversary, the devil. We must take the attitude "I hate the devil and he hates me. The feelings are mutual!" Spiritual friendly fire is when we use gossip, slaughter, competition to injure, hurt, or kill our fellow brothers and sisters in Christ without finding out the facts. Whether we witnessed it firsthand or not does not give us a right to place judgment or to speak about something concerning others. We have to keep in mind that we are not one another's enemy. "We seldom judge others by their actions and judge ourselves by our intentions" (https://www.modernservantleader.com/). If we would take that time to put a prayer on it, the church would impact the world at a greater degree. My mother would say, "A dog that brings a bone will carry a bone!" We all have been victims or perpetrators. I say, "This weapon, you can disarm yourself by simply putting a *prayer on it*!" The perimeters of the church must continue to be strengthened and guarded. I call it the SPP method – strengthen the perimeters with prayer. In the latter chapters, we will discuss this strategy in depth. A loaded gun only becomes a danger when it is fired!

Keep the Safety On

I went to a gun range with several friends, and the instructor pointed out a few imperative rules:

1. Keep your safety on until you're ready to fire.
2. Keep your gun pointed down range.
3. Always handle your weapon as if it is loaded.

Our words are powerful. *James 3:4-6, The Message Bible*, puts it this way: *"A bit in the mouth of a horse controls the whole horse. A small rudder on a huge ship in the hands of a skilled captain sets a course in the face of the strongest winds. A word out of your mouth may seem of no account, but it can accomplish nearly anything or destroy it!"* Set a watch over the doors of my lips (Psalm 141:3, KJV). We must be careful to keep the safety on our lips; our words are loaded. Watch what you release over your family, finances, future, and even your foes!

Military Friendly Fire

During World War II, it has been recorded that at least 21 percent of casualties were killed by friendly fire. Friendly fire means a weapon fired and coming from one's own side, especially fire that causes accidental injury or death to one's own force. On August 23, 2007, the United States Air Force F-15 called in to support British ground forces in Afghanistan to drop a bomb on those forces. Three privates of First Battalion, Royal Anglin Regiment, were killed, and two others were severely injured. The investigation revealed that the British air controller who called in the coordinates had not been given or issued a noise-cancelling headset, and he did the correct target coordinates, but in the confusion and stress of the battle, he incorrectly confirmed one wrong digit, mistakenly repeated by the pilot, and the bomb landed on British position (his own soldiers). The original target was one thousand meters away from the enemy (www.bbc.com). The coroner testified that the incident was caused by flawed application of procedures rather than individual errors or recklessness. The stress of the battle can cause many soldiers to be killed; injured, or severely wounded! We must remember that we are all on the Lord's side. Make sure we are not operating for the enemy by using defective application of words.

Active Shooter

According to the US Justice Department, an *active shooter* is a term that has been associated with an individual who has malicious intent and is actively engaged in killing or attempting to kill people in a confined or populated area. In most cases, active shooters use firearms, and there is no pattern or method to their selection of victims. Most active shooters have triggers, which may be stemmed from anger, loss of job, radically motived, emotional and mental disturbances, and some may be motivated by popularity (www.dhs.gov/activeshooter).

On the other hand, when we release the word of God against the kingdom of darkness, we are active shooters. We release the Lord's arrow of victory over our lives, families, and situations. During Elisha's final prophecy, he gave instructions to the king to open the east window, so the king opened it. "Shoot," Elisha said, and the king shot, then Elisha said, *"That is the arrow of the Lord's victory, the arrow of victory against Aram. You will completely defeat the Arameans at Aphek"* (2 Kings 13:17, God's Word Translation). Instead of releasing death, release life!

CHAPTER SEVEN

Don't Just Stand There. Pray Something.

THE DEADLIEST WEAPON EVER: PRAYER

First of all, then, I urge that petitions, prayers, intercessions, and thanksgiving be offered on behalf of all men.

—1 Timothy 2:1, Berean Study Bible

Prayer is the most important part of a believer's walk with God. Prayer is a spiritual transaction between God and man. It is not only dialogue, but also communication. Dialogue is written or spoken conversational exchange between two or more people. Communication is the imparting or exchanging of information or news. It is sending or receiving information (www.dictionary.com, *Holman's Bible Dictionary*). When we dialogue, it is information being shared back and forth, as we pray to God. If we have a listening heart, he is able to speak back to us. Communication takes the object of prayer to an entirely new level. In your prayer time, God imparts and downloads into your spirit and sometimes shows you things to come.

Petitions, according to the Strong's Greek (1162), means to pray for a specific felt need or heartfelt need arising out of deep personal need (a sense of lack/want). We are to petition God on a regular basis. The Bible says, *"Be careful for nothing, but in everything by prayer and supplication with thanksgiving let your requests be made known unto God" (Philippians 4:6, KJV).* Throughout the Bible, men and women of God brought their request to God, and he responded. Jesus spent countless hours in prayer daily, which depicts the importance of prayer to the believer. It is recorded that Jesus's life was surrounding around prayer and fasting. He had a passion for prayer. His desire to obey the will of God drew him to a place of prayer. His persistence in prayer showed his commitment to the Father. Jesus's heart and love for God caused him to pursue God with everything in him. During his time in prayer, God reveals to him his next assignment. Our foundation of prayer is instrumental during these perilous times. We must make it a habit to implement the following:

- Spend time with God daily.
- Include God in every decision (not just major ones).
- Always pray after God uses you for his glory (so you don't get high-minded or puff up).
- Set aside time just to thank him. There are times when I spend hours just thanking him for who he is and what he has done. Get a thank-you chair. Every time you sit in the chair, let it be a reminder to tell him thank you!
- Pray for your spiritual leaders, government, nation, family, and friends!
- Never forget to prayer for yourself!

In Luke 18:1, Jesus gives a parable to the disciples about a widow who was consistent and persistent in coming before an unjust judge with her request for justice from her adversary. He teaches the significance of the impact of what prayer does. It can change the mind of the wicked, reverse the outcome, and call God on the scene. The widow refused to take no for an answer. She did not care that he did not regard God or man, but she was not going to stop until she got her desired result. As believers, we must have this kind of spiritual tenacity and bravery. The widow knew what she was entitled to and demanded her property, and more than anything else, her faith was intact. Her faith calls God to the rescue. *"But without faith it is impossible to please him; for he that cometh to God must believe that he is, and that he is a rewarder of them that diligently seek him" (Hebrew 11:6, KJV).*

Subsequently, the Bible gives a detailed description of the need for the armor of God. It explains that we should pray in the spirit at all times, with every kind of prayer and petition. *To this end, stay alert with all perseverance in your prayers for all saints (Berean Study Bible). Never stop praying, especially for others. Always pray by the power of the Spirit. Stay alert and keep praying for God's people (Ephesians 6-18, Contemporary English Version).* Praying in the spirit is one of my favorite things to do because, as stated earlier, the enemy cannot comprehend or intercept our prayers. I call it my secret weapon. When we pray under the unction of the Holy Spirit, we pray with the direction, guidance, and influence according to the word and will of God. Praying in the spirit is one of the most deadly and effective weapons of mass destruction that is under-utilized in the body of Christ. *The word of God gives us clear understanding that when we don't know what to pray the holy spirit makes intercession for us with groaning which cannot be uttered and help our weakness (Romans 8:26, KJV).* The

Holy Spirit prays the mind of God. *But you, beloved, build yourself up on [the foundation of] your most holy faith [continually progress, rise like an edifice higher and higher], pray in the Holy Spirit and keep yourselves in the love of God, waiting anxiously and looking forward to the mercy of our Lord Jesus Christ [which will bring you] to eternal life (Jude 1:20-21, The Message Bible).* Praying in the Holy Spirit is divine assistance.

What Prayer Did for Me and in Me

My salvation and prayer life came as a result of almost losing my daughter. She was six weeks old and born in a German hospital. When we took her home, she seems to be a healthy baby girl. Several days before she turned six weeks, we had a well-baby checkup. As I waited in the doctor's office, I observed a poster on the wall showing how to give infants cardiopulmonary resuscitation (CPR). As I quickly dismissed it, I heard the voice of God say, "Read it and remember it!" At this time, I was not saved but grew up in church and somehow knew the voice of God. Little did I know this information would save my daughter's life. The next day I placed my daughter down for a nap in a German crib. If you know anything about them, they are made of natural wood and lined with a down comforter fitted to lay the baby on. My landlord had given us the crib to use before my daughter was born. About thirty minutes after I put her down for a nap, she began crying. I got up and checked on her, and she was fine but did not stop crying. I thought to myself she will be all right and eventually go back to sleep. All of a sudden, she stopped crying, and I was relieved, but the voice of the Lord spoke and said, "Check her now!" I went in the room, and she was gray and not breathing. I began to scream, and my husband snatched her out of my arms and begin to do adult CPR on her; however, it was ineffective. I screamed, "Lord, don't take my baby now!" Suddenly, the poster from the doctor's office appeared in front of me (in midair), and I begin reading it! Eventually, my daughter took a deep breath, and my husband told me to open the window and let her breath fresh air. When I got to the army hospital, the doctors and nurses came running outside and grabbed my baby out of my arms. Over a period of several days, she went through series of test to determine if she would be mentally retarded. Several days later, we were taken in an ambulance to a German specialist. The entire time I remember praying that the test would come out normal. I prayed to God and asked him to please spare my daughter of any side effects. This was the beginning of my prayer life with God and my testimony that God is faithful! As a result of this, I got saved nine months later!

The Power of Intercession

In Genesis 18:23, Abraham interceded that God would not destroy Sodom and Gomorrah. Abraham asked God to spare the land for fifty souls, and eventually, his request was changed to ten. God knew that there was not fifty righteous people in the land but allowed Abraham to keep petitioning him on their behalf. I call this a spiritual negotiation. My question to God, "Why didn't you tell him that there were not fifty righteous?" It was a matter of faith! God wanted Abraham to exercise his faith and trust him, that if he continues to ask, that he would give him his heart's desire! Abraham had a special burden for the land because Lot, his nephew, lived there. Like Abraham, we must intercede for our family, friends, neighbors, and country and ask God to have mercy on them and save their souls. All throughout the Bible, there is clear evidence that prayer changes things, but it also changes people. It is never too soon, too late, or too far gone to pray for anyone or anything. God can step in at any given moment and turn the tables. I am a living witness, it took twenty-one years of fasting and prayer, but God saved my husband three days before he passed! Your prayer may be the answer to someone's problem!

Now discharge your weapon!

A prayer for the readers and receivers!

Father, in the name of Jesus, I thank you for the readers of this book. May their life be forever changed, and may it be used to help others understand the power of prayer. Father, thank you so much for allowing this book to land in the hand and heart of each believer. May their life be catapulted, impacted, shifted, and uplifted for your glory, and may your anointing rest upon their life, that the kingdom of God will be increased in excellence! In the name of Jesus!

A prayer for your loved ones!

Father, in the name of Jesus, I pray that you would touch the heart of (insert name), my loved one. Father, take the heart of stone and put in a heart of clay (Ezekiel 36:26, KJV). Father, you declared in your word that you would save my entire household. Now, Father, I pray that you would move by the power of your word. Go down into the recesses of their heart and heal, deliver, set free every broken place, wounded place, and place of abandonment and rejection. I decree that the soul of (insert name) belong to you, in the name of Jesus! I stand in faith on your word because grass may wither and flower may fade but your word will stand forever. I thank you that your word will not return until you void it, but it will accomplish that for which it was sent. In the name of Jesus!

ABC of Salvation!

Father, I acknowledge that I am a sinner and need a savior. I *ask* that you forgive me of my sin and wash me clean. I *believe* that Jesus Christ died for my sins and rose on the third day. You said, if I *confess* with my mouth that Jesus is Lord and believe in my heart that God raised Jesus from the dead, that I shall be saved. For with the heart man believeth unto righteousness and with the mouth confession is made unto salvation, according to Romans 10:9-10 (KJV). I accept you into my heart and receive you as my Lord and Savior! In the name of Jesus!

Welcome to the kingdom of God, my brother or sister! May God keep and bless! Now find you a good church home and pray for God to show you his purpose and plan for your life!

References

Amplified Bible
Christian Standard Bible
Darby's Bible Synopsis
Darby Bible Translation
Geneva Study Bible
Holman Christian Standard Dictionary
https://en.wikipedia.org/wiki/Royal_Anglian_Regiment
https://goarmy.com
https://military.com
https://nationalarchives.gov.uk/
King James Bible
Matthew Henry Commentaries
Matthew Henry Concise
New International Version
New King James Bible
New Living Translation
Open Bible
Strong Concordance
The Message Bible
The Parallel Bible

The Truth Renaissance, "When God Wants to Drill a Man," https://thetruthrenaissance.wordpress.com/.

www.army.com

www.army.mod.uk/news-and-events/

www.bbc.com

www.BibleGateway.com

www.Biblehub.com

www.BibleStudyTools.com

www.britannica.com

www.dhs.gov/activeshooter

www.dictionary.com

www.harriet-tubman.org

www.merriam-webster.com/

www.military.com

www.royalanglianregiment.com/news/association-suffolk-minden-day/

www.usconcealedcarry.com

www.wearethemighty.com.

CPSIA information can be obtained
at www.ICGtesting.com
Printed in the USA
BVHW032009301220
596689BV00005B/45